CONTENTS

SCHOOL'S IN

Going to school is something that you take for granted. One day you're quite happy playing at home, the next you're sitting at a desk with a pencil in your hand. But what is school? How would you describe it to an alien who has just landed – zap! whoosh! pop! – in your classroom?

This is what the pupils in this school would tell the alien.

"You go to school to learn but it's also where you learn how to get along with other kids and adults."

Jason

"At school you learn the things that will help you when you're older and want to get a job. It's fun except for doing homework and tests."

Fashed

"It's where kids go to learn to read and write and to do maths. But the art and music lessons are the best."

Camille

"If it wasn't for the teachers at school I wouldn't be able to read and write or use new technology. I met all my friends at school."

Akiko

"School is about learning how to learn. If you know how to work things out for yourself then you become more independent."

Lucy

"School is like a family. We care for each other, help each other and follow the rules. We even have chores to do. At school the chores are learning to listen, think and work."

Mrs Hassim, class teacher

"Learning information and skills are just two things that are done at school. The most important thing that I can share with my class is learning respect for other people and for themselves."

Mrs O'Brien, class teacher

THE BIG QUESTIONS

What would happen if there were no schools? OK, so teachers wouldn't have much to do, but what else?

What would you be doing?

Would it change your future?

WHAT'S HOMEWORK?

WHERE HAVE YOU BEEN? LOST IN SPACE OR SOMETHING?

It's your turn to give the visiting alien the low-down on your school.

WHAT'S IN IT FOR ME?

Do you see school like a football match where it's the Terrible Teachers versus the Poor Pupils? Or do you have a sneaking suspicion that you and the teachers are playing for the same team?

To find out if you and your school have something in common, find answers to these questions using the answers given in the coloured panels. You can use each answer as many times as you like.

Is my teacher an angel or a monster?

Be patient

Be helpful

Be honest

Show respect

Be tolerant

Treat everyone equally

Question 1:
What can school and teachers do for you?

Question 2:
What can you do for your school and teachers?

Be fair

Be friendly

Be polite

Consider each other's needs

Be understanding and caring

Are you, your school and teachers on the same team? Does it help you to learn, meet friends and play if the school environment is happy and safe? What would happen if you and your teachers did not show respect towards each other?

SCHOOL RECIPE

Create a recipe for a good school using these ingredients. You can use some or all of the ingredients and in any quantity you like.
☺ Healthy and safe environment
☺ Tolerance for all beliefs and cultures
☺ Respect for each other
☺ Lots of enthusiasm
☺ A willingness to learn and to teach
☺ Patience and understanding
☺ Heaps of sports equipment
☺ No homework
☺ Stacks of computers and books
☺ No bullying
☺ Lots of laughs and happy people
☺ No detentions
    ☺ No rules
      ☺ Lots of helpful, caring people

Does your recipe for a good school sound like your school?

How is it different?

What ingredients are missing from your school or from the recipe?

THE BIG QUESTIONS

Can each person in a school help make it a better place?

Have you done anything to make your school a better place?

R U L E S
WHAT A JOKE!

Why are there rules about everything at school? There are rules about punctuality, about behaviour, about what you can and can't wear; there may even a rule about when you can go to the toilet. But are rules just a joke; things that take the fun out of fun, or are they there to help everyone?

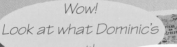

DOMINIC'S BAD DAY

Wow! Look at what Dominic's got!

Can I have a go?

Computer games are banned at school.

Dumb rule!

Hide it, Dominic. Teacher's coming.

Because Dominic broke a rule by bringing a valuable item to school, we've got a theft, nasty accusations, bad feelings and a real thief to deal with. This class is on lunchtime detention until everything's sorted out.

LATER

It's gone! Someone's taken it. Was it Shane? He wanted to have a go.

What's going on?

Give it back.

I didn't touch it. I swear.

OK; if you didn't take it, who did?

RULES FOR A REASON

RAISE YOUR HAND TO ASK A QUESTION

Why have a rule about what can and can't be brought into school?
* Is it a good rule or a bad rule?
* How does Dominic feel about the rule now?
* Is it fair that the whole class is being punished?
* What other rules have been broken?
* How could you help the class sort out its problems?

If you're in trouble because you've broken a rule or if you don't understand the purpose of a rule, your school rules may seem unfair or just plain silly.

Some rules help you, your friends and teachers work together, others protect everyone's rights and property, and some rules are for safety. What are the purposes of these rules?

NO RUNNING IN THE CORRIDORS; WALK ON THE LEFT

NO JEWELLERY TO BE WORN WHEN PLAYING SPORTS

BE PUNCTUAL

IF AN ALARM SOUNDS, GO STRAIGHT TO YOUR CLASS MEETING AREA IN THE PLAYGROUND

VISITORS MUST SIGN IN AT THE OFFICE AND WEAR A BADGE

A TICKING OFF

Give yourself a tick for each 'yes' answer.
- ✔ Do you know your school's rules?
- ✔ Who wrote the rules?
- ✔ Can they be changed?
- ✔ Do rules have to be fair and have a purpose?

If you answered 'no' to any questions, become a detective and find out about your school's rules.

THE BIG QUESTION

What would happen if there were no rules at school?

DON'T PICK ON ME!

Getting along with everyone at school is easier to say than to do. Sometimes you fall out with your friends, have disagreements with others at break time and it all goes wrong. Chances are that these normal hassles will be forgotten or solved with a few friendly words or an apology.

But sometimes, trouble happens and then keeps on happening. If you or someone you know is being picked on – being treated badly or differently from everyone else – then, sadly, bullying has raised its ugly head.

Bullying means lots of things. Different bullying situations are shown in these photos. While you look at them, describe what's happening and how you would feel if they were happening to you.

"My supposed friends have been giving me the cold shoulder for ages. I've asked them why, but they say nothing and turn away from me. Aren't I good enough to be their friend?"

Ahmed

"The names she calls me are horrible, but what really upsets me is how mean she looks when she turns nasty. I have nightmares about her."

Ami

"She thought that poking things in my back and dropping rubbers down my shirt was just a bit of fun. The first time it was, but not every day since."

Janet

"Everyone laughed the first time she dropped a rubber down Janet's back, but she won't stop. Janet just put up with this teasing so I told the teacher."

Brett

"Ahmed and those three guys were best mates then for no reason they gave him the silent treatment. Ahmed is so sad. He hangs around with us now but I know he misses them."

Debs

"Everyone loses their cool sometimes, but that shouting is dead scary. When it happens, Ami and everyone else pretend they can't hear her. When she's gone, Ami cries."

Pru

"We're not in the same year, I don't think she knows my name and I've never done anything to her, but she goes out of her way to accidentally-on-purpose shove me." Lyn

"The practical jokes have been going on for weeks. I feel everyone's watching to see what I'll do. I'm now too frightened to open my lunch box." Shaun

"When we're moving around the school, I'm going to try and stick close to Lyn. The shoving's bad enough, but what if it gets worse?" Jeanette

"When they found out that Shaun was terrified of spiders, they put a dead one in his lunch box. It's out of hand now and Shaun is totally paranoid. I'm going with him to see the headteacher." Thomas

WHAT IS BULLYING?

Saying horrible things (verbal abuse)

Pushing, shoving or worse (physical abuse)

Treating someone differently to everyone else (discrimination)

Teasing, frightening and excluding someone (emotional abuse)

WHY DO KIDS BECOME BULLIES?

Bullies are basically cowards who try to make themselves look 'big' by picking on someone. Bullies are sad and pathetic people and don't you ever forget it!

WHAT HAPPENS TO SOMEONE WHO'S BULLIED?

It can make them feel like a victim who is helpless and has no control over what's happening. They feel very bad about themselves, lose their confidence and feel worthless. Sounds serious? You bet! The effects of bullying can last for years.

Bullying has to be stopped. What can be done? There's lots that is already being done, but there are important jobs for you and your friends to do. Turn to the next page to find out more.

11

CLASS ACTION!

If something bad is happening people often group together to do something about it. Organizations start because a few people decide to take action on say, environmental issues or injustice. At school, you may have already banded together to organize a fund-raising event for a charity.

If problems like bullying, litter, vandalism, stealing, discrimination or drug-taking are affecting your school, ask your teacher if your class could talk about it. From this discussion you and your classmates could come up with ideas of how to solve the problem.

Taking issue

This class are concerned about bullying so they've had a talk about it with their teacher. They all agree that something has to be done to help anyone being bullied and that bullying has to be stopped. Here are their ideas:

This is the poster that one class wrote:

FRIENDS' RULES ...

① Be a good friend to the person being bullied – stay with them.

② Don't confront or threaten the bullies.

③ Don't look scared, don't react; stand up tall and walk away.

④ Insist that your friend tell an adult NOW! If they won't, tell them that you will do it for them.

⑤ Do something different – join a school club, play in a different area of the playground, sit with another class at lunch, find new friends to hang around with.

⑥ Don't do anything to encourage the bullies.

⑦ No one deserves to be bullied ... ever!

How about doing a special school assembly?

Could we get someone in to talk to us?

I could write a rap or a song.

We could design posters!

LET'S HAVE A HEATED DEBATE!

Another way to raise issues among your class is to have a debate. A debate is when one group in the class talks in favour of a topic and another group talks against it. The rest of the class decide which group made the stronger argument.

In a debate there are rules about how long you can talk, so ask if your teacher can chair the debate. You could also debate a hot school topic among your friends.

Here are some ideas for a class debate:

Are school uniforms good or bad ?

Should sport and P.E. be compulsory?

Should you be able to wear make-up to school?

Is there too much homework?

What works – reward or punishment?

THE BIG QUESTION

Should you try to help solve problems at your school or just leave it to the teachers?

I could write a play about it and we could perform it during lunchtime.

We could write a set of rules about it!

We could get computer games or books about it.

I could do a questionnaire for everyone to answer.

We could start a school newspaper.

Where's your self-respect?

Before you start searching for it, do you know what you're actually looking for? Self-respect is liking yourself and being honest with yourself (and with everyone else). You know your good points and your not-so-good-points, and you'd never do anything to hurt yourself or your amazing potential.

James is the new boy at school and he's anxious to make friends. Read on to see how James gets on.

JAMES AND THE GIANT FIB

Was James honest with himself?
Was he honest with his new friends?
Do you think James has self-respect?
Would it have mattered if James had told Nelson that he couldn't skate?

Look at Maria's diary to show the difference that high esteem and self-respect make to how you feel.

Dear Diary,

I can't believe it - I got 10 out of 10 for a maths test today. What's more - I got a part in the school play and that kid who used to give me grief has asked me to the cinema. Doesn't seem that long ago when I was telling you how bad everything was, how nobody liked me, how much trouble I was in, blah, blah, blah. I really didn't like myself then, did I? I thought I was pretty useless, so I acted useless and then people told me how useless I was, so I really must have been useless then.

I think I'd still be in trouble if that new art teacher hadn't boosted my confidence by entering my painting in the competition. What a buzz! That's all for today, I've got to choose something to wear. (I'm going out, you know.)   Maria

GETTING SOME SELF-RESPECT

Everyone goofs-up, flunks a test, has a downer day with friends, gets into trouble – but if you've got self-respect you'll get over it and learn from it. Don't let one bad thing ruin everything else you've got going for you.

To remind yourself that you're a great example of the human race, ask yourself these questions. Honest answers only, please.

1 What are your three favourite subjects?
2 Which is your best subject or school activity?
3 What can you do now that you couldn't do last year?
4 What do you want to be able to do next year?
5 How have you helped others at school?

"When I'm sad, I look at myself in the mirror – it's impossible not to smile."   Tobias

"To remind myself that I'm pretty good, I read my ballet reports. They make me feel so good."   Rebecca

"Maths is a nightmare, so after I've done it I reward myself with a session on the computer. Now that's where I'm ace!"   Robin

YOUR RESPECT IS SHOWING

You can show respect to your friends and to the staff and teachers at school in lots of ways. A friendly and polite 'good morning' is always a good start. The important thing is, that once you show respect for someone, they'll show their respect for you.

Answer these questions to find how you rate on respect.

1. A lot of girls in your class cover their hair with a scarf. Do you ...
a) know that it is part of their religion and respect their beliefs?
b) think, great way to hide a bad hair day?
c) make fun of them?

2. The caretaker is carrying boxes through the school. Do you ...
a) say hello and open the door for him?
b) hope the boxes contain the new sports equipment?
c) rush past knocking the boxes to the ground?

3. Your new teacher has asked the class to pay attention. Do you ...
a) stop what you're doing and look at her?
b) think, "what, new teacher?"
c) raise your voice so that you can be heard over the teacher?

4. The parent of a boy in your class has died. When the boy returns to school, do you ...
a) say how sorry you are and offer to help him catch up on work?
b) go out of your way to avoid him?
c) tell him to cheer up and tell a sick joke?

5. You're working on the school computer when suddenly it crashes big time. Do you ...

a) immediately tell the teacher?

b) sneak away and say nothing?

c) wildly push every button and then thump it?

HOW DID YOU DO?

Mostly As – Your respect is definitely showing for beliefs and cultures different to your own, for people (teachers are people, you know) and their feelings, and for your school environment. Keep it up!

Mostly Bs – It's not that you've got no respect (it's there somewhere) but more that you just don't seem to care. Join the human race!

Mostly Cs – Wow, there's some work to be done here. Try and put yourself in, say, the new teacher's shoes. How would you feel about someone who is so disrespectful and rude?

Show your respect for

All people by treating them fairly and politely.

The environment and property by doing them no harm.

Different beliefs and cultures by learning about them.

People's feelings by being honest and sensitive.

LEARNING RESPECT

Some kids say and do disrespectful things because they are frightened or fearful of people that are unfamiliar or situations that they don't understand. If they took the time to ask questions and learn – say about different religions, cultures, ways of living – they would be more understanding, less fearful and could show their respect.

THE BIG QUESTIONS

Do you respect your friends at school?

How do you show it?

17

On your best behaviour

Just what does 'on your best behaviour' mean? You hear it all the time – a parent will say it as you walk into school, your teacher will say it when they leave you alone in the class for a micro-second, and the headteacher will command it of you when your class goes on an outing. But what does it mean? Here's what some pupils think.

"It means being quiet, not annoying anyone and not telling fibs." Jo

"When we go on outings, being on our best behaviour means walking in lines with a partner, doing what you're told, not running off, not talking to strangers, getting on the bus and not leaving any rubbish behind." Nathalie

"At school it means getting on with work quietly. It's about being polite, responsible, quiet and not running or causing trouble." Euan

"It means being on our best behaviour in assemblies or when we have visitors so that the school looks its best." Nicky

There's a lot to this 'best behaviour' stuff. Look at this photo story and give this class marks out of ten for behaviour.

CLASS MISBEHAVES

WHAT WILL THE TEACHER DO WHEN HE RETURNS?

Will he be upset that he can't trust them or angry that they disobeyed him?

What are the benefits of being trusted and responsible?

THE BIG QUESTIONS

Is it important to do as you're told?

What could happen if everyone ignored what they were asked to do?

19

TWO'S COMPANY, THREE'S A CROWD

Art lessons, football matches and science experiments are great, but one of the best things about school is that it is a good place to make friends. You and your friends may have met on your very first day at school and your friendships may continue for years. School friendships are very important, which is why it's so awful when they go wrong.

What has happened between Jade, Kate and Lucy?
Why does Lucy play the trick on Kate?
Will these three ever be good friends?
Read what Jade, Lucy and Kate have to say.

"I like to have lots of friends but I suppose my special friends are Kate and Lucy. I don't want to have to choose between them – I like them both."

Jade

"When Lucy's not around, Jade and I hang out with a whole bunch of friends. There's no hassle."

Kate

"Kate and I have been friends for ages, but now I want to be best friends with Jade. Kate should try and find some new friends."

Lucy

Friendships – great when they're working, so sad when they aren't. Can you think of how these three could work out their problem? Should they ask the teacher to help them? Should the three of them sit down and talk about it? Should it be Kate or Lucy that backs off?

PSST. WANNA HEAR SOME GOSS ABOUT JIM?

JIM

Killer gossip

Talking behind each other's backs, spreading nasty rumours and telling tales will ruin friendships in double-quick time. Gossip destroys trust, and once trust is gone an honest friendship is impossible. Leave gossip to the soaps on TV; in real life, honest face-to-face talking is the way to go.

How to keep friendships blooming

1. Be yourself – if you try to live up to the expectations of others, it will be a disaster. Anyway, you're such a great person, why hide it?

2. Be honest – if something is going wrong, talk about it. You should be able to talk to a good friend face-to-face (not behind their back) about anything!

3. Be trusting – don't become jealous if a friend spends time with someone else. If jealousy creeps in, it's time your self-respect had a check-up!

4. Be independent – no one wants to hang around with a copy-cat friend who says and does everything that you say or do. Copy-cat friends are as annoying as copy-cat brothers and sisters!

5. Be open – even if you and your friends are very close it doesn't mean that you can't get out there and mingle or welcome others in.

6. Be supportive – to any friend who's going through a bad patch.

7. Be ready to move on – as you grow and change, so will your friendships. Don't fight it by hanging onto the friendship, let go.

THE GANG'S ALL HERE

There are lots of wild animals who herd in large numbers as a way of protecting themselves, their territory and their food. And if an animal from another herd tries to join or wanders on to their territory to find food, he is quickly sent on his way. Sometimes gangs of schoolfriends behave in just the same way. They stay in a gang because they feel safe and because of their number, they feel strong. Being in a gang can be great, but sometimes it's not.

"I like hanging around with a lot of kids. We do things together, have heaps of fun, help each other and we stand up for each other."

Nathaniel

"Our gang was the most popular one – everyone wanted to join it, but we didn't let anyone. We all got on really well, knew everything about each other, so why muck up a good thing?"

Anita

"I used to hang around with this bunch of kids but when I wanted the new boy in our class to become one of the gang, they said no. That's when I realized that my friends really weren't very nice and I left. They won't talk to me now."

Robbie

"There was the gang of kids who always hung around together, you never saw them apart. They sort of controlled a part of the playground and they'd only let you play there if they liked you or you did something for them."

Andy

"I've got lots of friends but we all move about, we don't always hang around together. But if I'm in trouble or a bit sad, they all come to help me."

Katherine

"Liz is the leader of a gang and all the kids treat her like she's queen or something. I think she's a power-freak and the kids, pathetic."

Dave

"Our class used to be divided in two. There were the goody-goody kids in one gang, and the slackers in another. If you didn't want to join either of them, they both made your life a misery."

Sam and Maria

When you're in a gang, it's hard to tell if you're together because you really like each other and have lots in common, or just because it makes you feel secure, wanted and popular. Do this quiz to find out.

22

1. If the gang does something you don't agree with, do you ...
a) say nothing because you don't want to fall out with them?
b) go along because if it's OK with the others, it's OK with you?
c) stand up for yourself no matter what the consequences?

2. You decide to spend lunchbreak with some other friends. What does the gang do?
a) They talk about me behind my back.
b) I wouldn't hang around with any other kids and that's it.
c) They don't mind.

3. Do you have good friends who are not in the gang?
a) A few.
b) Of course not.
c) Lots of really good mates.

4. If the gang chucked you out because you 'aced' in a test, what would you do?
a) I'd be really upset and try to get back in with them.
b) If I 'aced' in a test, I'd keep it to myself.
c) Walk away; who needs friends like that?

So how did you do? Count up the number of A, B and C answers.

Mostly As
You feel safe in the group and you think you need them, but you don't really. Spend more time with other kids in the class.

Mostly Bs
The gang are holding you back big time. Start thinking for yourself before it's too late.

Mostly Cs
You can take them or leave them, you make your own decisions and have a large circle of friends.

THEY MADE ME DO IT

If someone has been made to do something – possibly something bad, against the rules, dangerous or illegal – because friends encouraged them to, then they have been under 'peer pressure'. Have you ever heard of anything like this happening to a friend or to someone at your school? Peer pressure makes some kids do things so that they are liked or accepted by a group. This is how it starts:

AMANDA'S DILEMMA

Are you up for some fun?

I suppose so. What is it?

Well, this is the plan. First we go and ...

Gemma and Lottie always have a good time. I'd really like to hang around with them.

Hey, Amanda, come over and join in. We've had a great idea.

What am I going to do? They won't let me hang around if I don't, and if I do there's bound to be trouble.

I'm not sure about this. It's breaking the rules and someone could get hurt.

Where's your sense of fun and adventure? I thought you'd be just the person to do it. Oh well, maybe someone else ...

What's Amanda going to do? She's got choices, but which one do you think she'll take?

CHOICE 1

CHOICE 2

Well, what did Amanda do? Did she make the right choice?

What would you have done in her position?

UNDER PRESSURE

Don't let anyone make you do something that you know is wrong. Friends who do this aren't friends at all, so you're better off without them. It's hard to stand up for what you think or believe, but harder to face the results of doing something you know is bad, dangerous or illegal.

A LITTLE LITTER GOES A LONG WAY

The first environment that you share with others is your home. The next is your school. You may never have thought about the school building, the playing field and the classroom as an 'environment', but it is one, and it needs to be cared for. And because your school is part of a larger environment – a suburb, a city, a village – everything that happens in your school affects the surrounding environment.

LITTER

Litter is not just about making a mess. It's also about safety, health and showing respect for people, property and for the natural environment.

Ask your teacher if you can make a poster to remind everyone to use the rubbish bins, not to waste paper and to look after the school and its grounds.

Alicia, Jessica and Matthew did this for their school.

Action stations

Conserving natural resources is as important at school as it is everywhere else. If you think that you and your classmates are concerned about the environment, why not start at school?

Dear Newsletter Editor

When we had to do a project about the environment, we decided to do 'our school'. We got some information about litter and recycling from the library and the local council.

We went around the school and saw that the rubbish bins weren't in the right places. They were too far away from where everyone had lunch, so rubbish was just left about or thrown in the garden. The bins didn't have lids and paper blew everywhere. There weren't any recycling bins for clean paper, newspaper or plastic.

We did a plan of the school and showed where rubbish and recycling bins should go. Then we drew a design for a bin that had a lid, was easy to empty and looked fun. We made the bin look like an alien. On the front of the bin was a sign: I have come to gobble your rubbish.

Our project got the highest marks in the class. The headteacher had the rubbish bins moved to the right positions and added some recycling bins. We haven't made the signs yet, but soon!

From Alicia, Jessica and Matthew.

THE BIG QUESTION

If you can't look after your school environment, what will happen to the wider environment?

27

EIGHT GREAT THINGS TO DO AT SCHOOL

As you drag yourself out of bed, pull on your school clothes and quickly shovel down spoonfuls of cereal, your only thought is making it to school on time. But how about sparing a minute to think of ways of spicing up your school day? It's easier than you think and the rewards are worth the tiny effort.

1 Smiling

You know that thing you do when your mouth turns up at the corners; it's a smile and it can move mountains, or at least wipe the grumpy expression off a tired teacher's face. A smile is highly infectious and has powerful side-effects. It makes everyone feel happy and friendly.

2 Listening

Another simple act, like smiling, that can really spice up your day. Listening is when you hear, take in, understand and act on what is being said. Listening is much more exciting than just hearing. Hearing is about as much fun as going to a football match and sitting behind an enormous pillar – you miss most of the moves. Listening is all about being there and catching every second of exciting action.

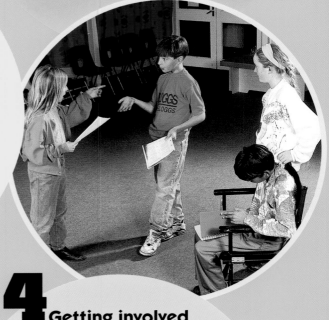

3 Doing a good deed

Make a promise to yourself that every day at school you will do a good deed without being asked and without seeking praise. A good deed could be binning litter in the playground, comforting someone who's had a fall, talking to someone who is standing alone, letting someone else have the last serving of chips at lunch. There's no end of good deeds to be done.

4 Getting involved

You can sit on the sidelines of school life (boring!) or you can get involved and have some fun. Join a sports team or school club, or better still, start one. You and some friends could organize an event for charity, or combine your talents and put on a performance at a class or school assembly.

5 Sweating it out

Do you know why Jack and Jill tumbled down the hill? Because all work (carrying buckets) and no play is boring. Though you may groan when it's time to change for P.E, gym, games or team sports, it's important to get some exercise. Not only does it make you feel better, exercise wakes up your brain and team sports teach you heaps about getting along with others, working together, leadership and about being a 'good sport'.

6 Share-and-tell

In many schools share-and-tell is about what everyone did at the weekend, a story about a sick hamster or showing off road rash from an in-line skating slam. Why not lighten it up by sharing a great joke and a laugh. Happy kids are supposed to laugh 50 times a days and happy adults (that includes teachers), six times a day. Keep your friends and teachers happy and healthy by giving them something to laugh about.

8 Chilling out

School's not perfect; but getting angry, sulking and giving up won't solve anything. If things are getting you down, you just have to find somewhere quiet and imagine you're in a favourite place (it could be at home or somewhere you've been on holiday) and doing something you really like. Really throw yourself into this wonderful daydream. When you're overflowing with happy thoughts and there's a smile on your face, lock back into orbit with school. You'll feel much better and be able to sort out any problems.

7 Being positive

This is not about being positive that school is a drag, it's about being positive that you are doing your best. If you're just coasting along and doing the minimum, then school will be a drag. Up your attitude and your school day will be something you'll look forward to. Promise!

Glossary

Belief Something you believe in. It may be a belief in a religion or something that you feel is right.

Bullying Teasing, frightening, threatening or hurting someone. It is often done by a gang that picks on one person.

Discrimination Treating someone differently to everyone else because of the way they look, what they wear, what they do, where they live or what they believe in. New children in school are often treated differently until everyone gets to know them.

Gang A group of children or young people. One type of gang seems to get along with everyone and causes no trouble. The other sort of gang seems set on throwing its weight around and causing trouble.

Peer pressure When children of your age try to make you do something that you don't want to do. They may tease you, call you names or give you the cold shoulder unless you do as they want.

Respect Listening to others and learning to understand their way of life and their beliefs. It is also about being polite to others.

Self-esteem Feeling good about yourself. It is like self-respect.

Self-respect Believing in yourself and your ideas and treating yourself well.

Tolerance Letting others have different beliefs and ways of living.

Vandalism Damaging and destroying property.

Books to read

Bullies, Bigmouths and So-called Friends by J. Alexander (Hodder Children's Books, 2006)

Girl World by Theresa Cheung (Hodder Children's Books, 2005)

Staying Cool, Surviving School by Roise Rushton (Puffin, 1995)

Talking About: Bullying by Bruce Sanders (Franklin Watts, 2003)

Why do people bully? by Adam Hibbert (Wayland, 2006)

Wise Guides: Bullying by Michele Elliott (Hodder Children's Books, 2005)

Wise Guides: Exam Skills by Kate Brookes (Hodder Children's Books, 2005)

XY by Matt Whyman (Hodder Children's Books, 2002)

Useful contacts

If you are being bullied (or have any other school or family problems), tell an adult you trust. If the problem is not solved, call Childline (UK) on 0800 1111. Their telephone service is open 24-hours a day, the call is free and won't be listed on a telephone bill. You can also call the National Society for the Prevention of Cruelty to Children or its Scottish equivalent on 0800 800 5000. Call 1800 666 666 for the Irish Society for the Prevention of Cruelty to Children.

For brochures about keeping safe at school, when out and at home, contact Kidscape at 2 Grosvenor Gardens, London SW1 0DH or call 0207 730 3300.

Picture acknowledgements
All pictures belong to the Wayland Picture Library.

Index

behaviour 18-19
beliefs 16-17
bullying 7, 10-11, 12

charity work 12, 28
chilling out 29
conservation 26, 27

debate 13
discrimination 11

enthusiasm 7
environment 12, 17, 27
exercise 29

fear 17
friendships 14, 20-21, 22, 23, 25

gangs 22-3
gossip 21

honesty 6, 15, 17

independence 5, 21

laughs 7
leadership 29
listening 28
litter 26-7, 28

misbehaviour 19

peer pressure 24-5
physical abuse 11
politeness 6, 16, 17
positive attitude 29

problems 12

respect 6, 7, 16, 17, 26
responsibility 19

rights 9
rules 7, 8, 9, 24

safety 7, 9, 26
self-esteem 15, 30
self-respect 14, 15
sensitivity 17
share-and-tell 29
smiling 28

teachers 6, 7
teasing 11
trouble 9, 10
trust 19, 21

verbal abuse 11